A Field Guide to Fire

David Chorlton
Illustrations by Julie Comnick

FUTURECYCLE PRESS
www.futurecycle.org

Library of Congress Control Number: 2015942351

Copyright © 2015 David Chorlton
All Rights Reserved

Published by FutureCycle Press
Lexington, Kentucky, USA

ISBN 978-1-938853-38-8

This book was produced for the occasion
of the exhibition *Fires of Change,* a collaborative project
with the Southwest Fire Science Consortium, the Flagstaff
Arts Council, and the Landscape Conservation Initiative (LCI)
funded by the Joint Fires Sciences Program and
the National Endowment for the Arts.

Illustrations

- 12 Woolsey Fire
- 16 Roosevelt Fire
- 20 Outlet Fire
- 26 Dude Fire
- 28 Rodeo-Chediski Fire
- 32 Aspen Fire (North Rim Grand Canyon)
- 36 Range Fire
- 40 Wallow Fire
- 44 Doce Fire
- 48 Aspen Fire (Mt. Lemmon)
- 50 Slide Fire
- 52 Schultz Fire
- 56 Yarnell Hill Fire
- 60 Warm Fire

Poems

- 11 The Language of Trees
- 13 A Field Guide to Fire
- 27 Fire Enters its Time
- 29 Tree Rings
- 31 Ponderosa
- 33 The Winged Forest
- 41 Inside Fire
- 43 The First Day
- 45 Firemail
- 51 Fire Run
- 53 Sunlight and Ashes: Forest after Fire
- 61 Forest Oracle

Foreword

The fires we are most aware of are those which quickly become the stuff of spectacular coverage on television news, and whose destructive powers set us watching for information on their percentage of containment. As we learn how many acres of forest have been destroyed, it is understandable that fire gets a universally bad name, especially when we have, for the most part, little insight into the existing options for forest management. In September of 2014, Julie Comnick and I were part of the group of artists who were given the opportunity to learn exactly what fire can do, and what it has done historically, to help avoid the vast and disastrous burns that have become unnervingly frequent in recent years.

Under the auspices of the Southwest Fire Science Consortium and the Landscape Conservation Initiative, we toured relevant sites on the Kaibab Plateau, and later near Sedona, where the Slide Fire had burned that summer, learning the many different implications of the word "fire." The experience gave a scientific basis for the art that would be created afterwards and alerted me to the many species of fire that exist, and the help they offer, forests in need.

This study comes at a time when climate change has long been a reality, and it holds a special threat for the Southwest as the potential burn season begins earlier and ends later than it has before, and drought conditions have made the forests especially vulnerable to a fire that might be started by a lightning strike or a careless act. Looking back, by way of old newspapers from before Arizona became a state, I found plenty of reports of forest fires although none were of the magnitude of the worst from recent years. We have clearly entered a different age in which we can envision the most familiar scenes from nature disappearing or being changed beyond recognition. If fire is an agent capable of realizing our worst fears, it is also a force which, appropriately harnessed, can hold them at bay.

—David Chorlton

Illustrations

The drawings in *A Field Guide to Fire*, which depict recent Arizona wildfires, were rendered with charcoal samples personally collected from each fire site, using archived photographs as references.

While regular wildfire cycles are essential for the health of the ecosystem, they are frequently accompanied by negative public perception of wilderness devastation and human disaster. The increased size and severity of recent fires—due to suppression strategies that began over a century ago, and the continual drought and warming trends resulting from climate change—have taken toll on the environment and humans alike.

The use of charcoal, as an art medium, dates back to the earliest Paleolithic cave paintings. That it still prevails today (in a refined and compressed form) attests to charcoal's variety of applications and archival nature. Working with the unrefined, burnt remnants of Ponderosa Pine or Manzanita found at each wildfire site presented creative challenges such as achieving tonal range and detail on a small scale, and meeting contemporary expectations with an archaic medium.

Paired with David Chorlton's poetry, the objective of these drawings is to reverse the trajectory of public perception as viewers gain a renewed appreciation for the necessity of wildfire toward sustaining the longevity of our shared landscape.

—*Julie Comnick*

The Language of Trees

Before the mysteries
   a forest contains
      had been explained

it was claimed by those
   who lived close enough to know
      that trees talk

and all it takes to hear them
   is that you listen,
      you,

who come from far away
   and trust only
      a language you already understand.

Woolsey Fire
Incident Type: Wildfire
Cause: Lightning
Date: 2011
Location: North Rim Grand Canyon, Point Imperial, AZ
Size: 424 Acres
Vegetation: Ponderosa Pine / Dead and Down Logs from 2000 Outlet Fire
Management: Managed

A Field Guide to Fire

I   *Lightning*

> *The Navajo believes that if he comes within the influence of the flames he will absorb some of the essence of lightning, which will therefore be attracted to him and sooner or later will kill him.*
>
> —*The Coconino Sun,* August 11, 1900

When darkness turns electric
and the sky descends
to where the ponderosas stand,
fire writes its name on air
with lightning five times hotter
than the sun.
              One strike
sizzles; one strike bites
into bark; one strike sparks
a blaze; one strike holds back
and follows a man all his life,
waiting to have him know
the fate of trees.

II *Human Caused*

> *...he discovered that a man wearing about a No. 7 shoe, followed by a dog, had gone up the trail...and crossed over the ridge, setting fires as he went.*
>
> —*Williams News,* July 02, 1904

This one is lit by the spark
in a pyromaniac's eye

when the shadows inside him join hands
with the ones the trees cast

once the buildup of cone and dry needles
ignites and the beautiful burning

continues to calm a troubled soul until
it cannot be distinguished from smoke.

III   *Trackside Fire*

> *The fire is supposed to have originated from the spark*
> *of a logging train locomotive and was not discovered by rangers*
> *until it had gained great headway.*
>
> —*The Arizona Republican,* June 28, 1916

A warm light feels its way
through openings among the trees
where woodpeckers flash
black and red among the rays,
                        so used to hearing
the iron pulse pass by
they let it come and go without
a fuss, thinking as they must
that whatever happens
                        happens as
a consequence of nature, even
when a single drop of fire
turns into a conflagration.

Roosevelt Fire
Incident Type: Wildfire
Cause: Lightning
Date: 2007
Location: North Rim Grand Canyon, AZ
Size: 5,240 Acres
Vegetation: Ponderosa Pine
Management: Managed

IV   Camp Fire

*He came to Flagstaff Saturday and paid a fine
of $10 for carelessness.*

It happens while someone is looking away,
preparing to pack up and leave
the bluebirds behind, to have a new wind
clear their songs from his ears,
to carry the place's memory away
for future contemplation:
                              the embers
won't release the moment
and grow into a flame that reaches for
the departing man, who *remarked
as he left Judge Kidd's office,
"I'll sure be absolutely sure my campfire
is extinguished in the future."*

(Quotes from *The Williams News,* May 6, 1921)

V *Wildfire*

> *A wildfire differs from other fires by its extensive size,*
> *the speed at which it can spread out from its original source,*
> *its potential to change direction unexpectedly, and its ability*
> *to jump gaps such as roads, rivers and fire breaks.*
>
> —"The Science of Wildland Fire," National Interagency Fire Center

Beginning unobtrusively, this fire
climbs from fallen needles
when the forest floor is dry.
                          It likes
to hide while nobody notices
the first flame taste the pine cones
lying around it, and with an appetite
for more it rides a wind gust
until it reaches the crowns
of trees in its path, and takes
them without ever
looking back.
                Faster uphill
than down, it outruns
those who would chase it,
and spreads itself wide
                         so as to make
itself visible for miles
although from distance it is impossible
to see how
              it drinks grass,
                          chews trees,
and spits out broken boughs
                      when
even birdsong
          is burning.

VI *Spotting*

Spot ignition, a discontinuous fire spread mechanism, frequently overwhelms the fire suppression effort, breaching large barriers and firebreaks.

—*International Journal of Wildland Fire*, 2010

All it takes is the will
of fire to break out
of containment; just when
it would have us believe it is tired
and wants to settle down
it catches on an updraft
    and comes down across a stream
        or miles away
            the heart of a forest ablaze
                is contained in a flake
                    of smoldering ash.

Outlet Fire
Incident Type: Prescribed Fire - Converted to Wildfire
Cause: Management Ignited
Date: 2000
Location: North Rim Grand Canyon, Point Imperial, AZ
Size: 12,440 Acres
Vegetation: Ponderosa Pine / Mixed Conifer
Management: Suppressed

VII *Control*

> ...*the choice is not between two landscapes, one with
> and one without a human influence; it is between two ways of living,
> two ways of belonging to an ecosystem.*
>
> —William Cronon, 1983

The slow smoke rising
signals where a fire crawls
along the forest bed,
crackling as it burns
the recent history away
of how the seasons brought
more heat than rain
and left the layered kindling
for the next storm
to ignite. It follows every rise
or ditch, flowing low
and holding to its purpose
though it strains sometimes
to stay within its means
the way a wolf might do
when scenting prey
in two directions.

VIII *Crown Fire*

> *As a result of a century of grazing and fire suppression, millions of acres have such high tree densities that they remain vulnerable to high-intensity crown fires.*

—Peter Aleshire in *Payson Roundup,* February 12, 2013

A rippling at first, then
the crackle.
        (There's still
a chance the burning
will be stopped, still
a gap through which
to escape.)
        Now the fire
has confidence
and fuel to make it
strong.
        (Smoke blocks
all the light except
that which comes
from flames.)
        The time
it has taken these trees to grow tall
is marked by their
rings as they tighten
in the heat's grip.
        (A red roar
passes through, devouring
everything.)
        Ashes float down
from where once the jays
had lived next to
the sky.

IX *Breakfast*

> *About 10 o'clock Sunday morning May 18, Candelaria and three of his men on their way to their sheep range on the Apache Forest stopped for breakfast on the road northeast of Green's Peak.*
>
> —*The St. Johns Herald and Apache News,* May 29, 1913

In the shadow of a raven's call
herders listen to the sizzle and snap
in the pan before a spark

crackling out of control
makes them outrun the fire

on yesterday's energy.

X *Cigarette*

No one knows the origin of the fire but was probably caused by a cigarette stub fanned by the high wind.

—*The Coconino Sun,* July 12, 1912

With his back to the wind
and his collar turned up to protect
the match he strikes,
a smoker takes a drag
that tastes of wasted time
for a man with so much
work to do he doesn't wait
after tossing the stub,
he just holds the hat
tight
        to
              his
                      head.

XI *Mythological*

> *The Navajos have a tradition that long ago the God of Fire became sorely displeased with the people of the earth and that in his anger he set fire to the world, driving their ancestors to the cactus country of the south.*
>
> —*The Coconino Sun,* June 21, 1912

When time turns into wind
the trees stand helpless in its way.

With a wink from the Fire God's eye

flames rise in beauty
saying *Come with us, become change, become
light.* And all

is changed
because men dismissed every warning

and ran until there was nowhere
else to run to.

Dude Fire
Incident Type: Wildfire
Cause: Lightning
Date: 1990
Location: Mogollon Rim, AZ
Size: 28,000 Acres
Vegetation: Ponderosa Pine / Pine-Oak Woodland
Management: Suppressed
Structures Lost: 63
Deaths: 6

Fire Enters Its Time

After the Pleistocene shaded
    into the Holocene,
ice into warmth and monsoons,

an era began in which crops
    grew as the seasons allowed,
then Cabeza de Vaca

arrived with horses, smallpox,
    and apples, and later Anglos
herded sheep and cattle

and cut timber
    for building their towns
which burned easily

when, for example, a boiler
    exploded at two in the afternoon,
left the lives of three men

in ashes, and wrecked
    engine Number Two
of the S.F.P. & P. Railroad.

Rodeo-Chediski Fire
Incident Type: Wildfire
Cause: Human
Date: 2002
Location: Coconino / Gila / Navajo Counties, AZ
Size: 468,638 Acres
Vegetation: Ponderosa Pine / Pine-Oak / Juniper-Pinyon
Management: Suppressed
Structures Lost: 426

Tree Rings

This tree heard the coming of the railroad
and many nights it felt
an owl's claws on the branch where she held
the darkness tight, dropping bones
barely thicker than the needles onto which they fell.

~

In the waning hours of a dry season,
Major John Reese remarked that the people of the state
were to blame for its desert moving north because they
cut their forests down and let stock chew the grass
which once grew *high as a horse's back.*

~

After the gentleman from Oregon drove three hours
through the pines, beginning five o'clock one Sunday morning
in the year nineteen hundred, they heard him forecast that the day
was close at hand when *the national legislature would need
to afford relief as to the reclamation of the arid lands...*

~

Riding from the lake through country with no underbrush
a rich man from the east spurred his horse
and looked in wonder at the yellow flowers and grass
along the way to where the pines grew far apart
with the lowest branches high enough to let him pass.

~

On midsummer day in mid-century
the sun rose early, and began to warm the upper boughs
before it reached the bark beneath them
and warmed through to where the cambium
measured the circumference of drought.

~

The trains that carried lumber disappeared and others
came to replace them, always calling out along the rails
that passed the forest where ravens picked the highest snags
to sit and listen while the trains returned with goods
from China never stopping for anyone to ask about the future.

~

When it became the tallest pine among the pines
casting shadows onto silver earth in moonlight
it was marked for the bolt to strike it on the night
the forest stood for seconds in the white light that shone
through to the innermost ring among rings.

Ponderosa

This forest has roots
   ten thousand years deep
      and branches of lightning.
         Rain fell as needles here,
            drying on the ground
               where summers grew longer
                  and fire
                      found a home to return to.

Aspen Fire
Incident Type: Wildfire
Cause: Lightning
Date: 2009
Location: North Rim Grand Canyon, AZ
Size: 4,279 Acres
Vegetation: Ponderosa Pine
Management: Managed

The Winged Forest

I   *Flammulated Owl*

In the silence
that survived the Europeans

with their grazing herds,
a little owl

on a ponderosa pine
is a layer of the bark

until moths in fading light
come to the old growth space

where a long note
calls, and a claw

comes down to cut
the darkness open.

II *Long-legged Myotis*

Between the living
    trunks on summer nights
        bats navigate the clearings
           and flow in silence back
        to the snag among the pines
    where they cluster by day
behind a hinge of bark.

III *Northern Goshawk*

The Goshawk remembers
from its half-sheltered perch
the way the forest once
was open enough
for it to see where a grouse
or a rabbit had stopped for the second
it takes to dive two centuries

back and to grasp

the lost moment with talons

so sharp

they stop time.

Range Fire
Incident Type: Prescribed Fire
Cause: Management Ignited
Date: 2012
Location: North Rim Grand Canyon, AZ
Size: 2,316 Acres
Vegetation: Mixed Conifer
Management: Prescribed Fire

IV   *Common Raven*

Before and after fires
take what they need from the forest
and leave,

the shadows of the trees
take flight

as they fan into shapes
that rise through the canopy

into sky
where they spin on the light
and shine

all the way down
back to their roosts,

ruffled at the edges

weighing less than charcoal,

barely more than smoke.

V   *Spotted Owl*

The pines grow to the height
at which a hollow opens
where the broken parts allow
for the building of a nest.

>   An owl receives
>   every sound the night makes
>   and knows in the dark
>   where to swoop

for a mouse on the ground
when the ground is the weight
holding trees to the earth

while they age around the owls
who live in them.

VI *Red-naped Sapsucker*

The tapping in the aspens
       is the memory repeating
              of ponderosas standing here

before the fire.

Wallow Fire
Incident Type: Wildfire
Cause: Human
Date: 2011
Location: Apache National Forest near Alpine, AZ
Size: 538,049 Acres
Vegetation: Ponderosa Pine / Gamble Oak / Sagebrush
Management: Suppressed
Structures Lost: 72

Inside Fire

As water is to memory (the ocean
is history's first repository) fire
is imagination
starting lightly as a daydream
when a struck match
touches newspaper,
   a thumb flicks on
   the lighter just before
   a first long drag,
      or two sticks rub together
      the way they did
      to warm a cave
      in time before time
      became numbers:
it begins modestly, before
the flame deviates
from boredom to a misdemeanor
and whispers in the underbrush,
gathering strength
     but still just glowing
     in a forest's ancient darkness
   with a wisp
   of smoke as long
   as a fox's tail
   moving easily above the ground cover
     before anybody sees it,
     before it spreads,
     before it grows enough
to grip a tree's bark and jump
to the next one, spreading
bad news by word of mouth,
burning shadows as it brightens
to an otherworldly scarlet
while more smoke gathers

than the air has room for
and it appears that the land
is rising out of itself
    as molten light,
    energy
chasing ambition; now
it's the spy
who summoned an army to invade
and destroy what it can never
possess;
    crackle, snap, and the crash
    when heat explodes, the tall
    trunks aching
    and we still
      have far to go, breaking out
      of our routines,
      past containment,
brutal and beautiful
making a clear run
beyond survival.

The First Day

Lightning sparks a flame
   where trees hold up the sky;

      this is the one
         that breaks free

           and runs into the headlines.

On the ground it's cut and dig
   to clear a break

      but from the helicopter pinned overhead
        the pilot can see
          light and dark become one

            as the last chance of containment
           burns away

to a roar so hot

   it reaches

      the melting point of sound.

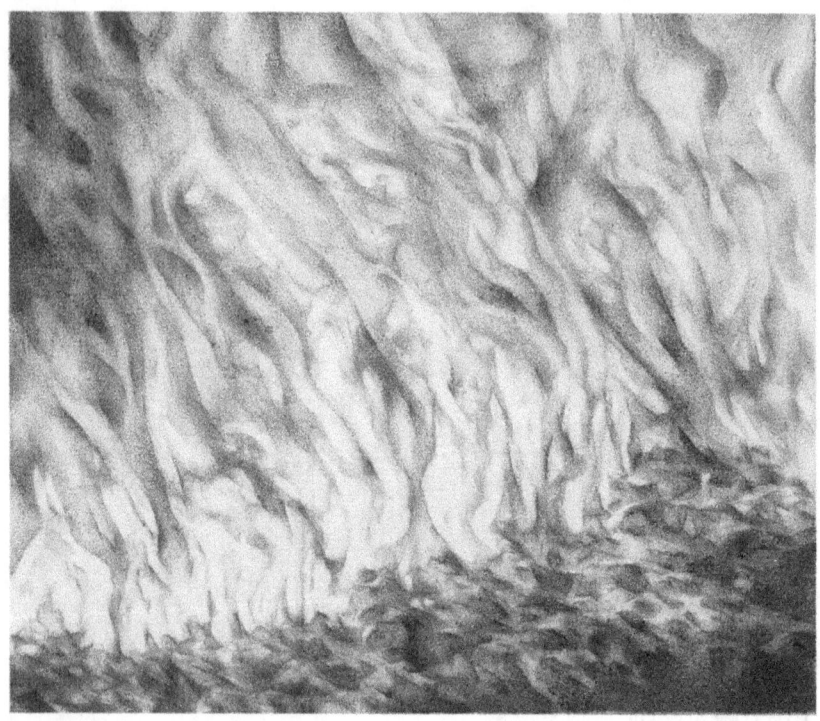

Doce Fire
Incident Type: Wildfire
Cause: Human
Date: 2013
Location: Granite Mountain Wilderness near Prescott, AZ
Size: 6,732 Acres
Vegetation: Chaparral
Management: Suppressed

Firemail

Before the scene was beautiful
with forest spitting flares
back into the brilliance
the clouds became
as they billowed into the night,
someone at a quiet desk
observed the land had been

> *Bone dry this year. Lots of fuel.*

and typed on a keyboard
that the stony peak
visible from the porch
was burning at the edges.

> *Is your place at risk?*

Few had an answer
outside of

> *sure sorry to hear about this*
> *and pray everyone is ok*

or watching from a distance safe
for now,

> *Awesome!*
> *Looks amazin'!*

as if they were watching
their own lives from within

the flames, where nothing more
could harm them, while the fire was

> *moving northeast.*
> *...given notice to be ready to evacuate*
> *at a moment's notice*

And the sleepless hours burned down
to morning coffee, with

> *Crews working in extreme terrain with very*
> *limited suitable locations to construct*
> *fire line capable of stopping the current*
> *and predicted fire behavior. Winds were*
> *gusty up to 40 mph early...*

A bear cub was running
at the roadside, while ravens
called to ravens through the haze.

> *Oh my gosh...glad she is safe.*
> *Hope it all turns out ok....*
> *thinking of you guys.*

Daylight struggled through the clouds
into canyons that two days earlier
had been so familiar
nobody ever noticed how
they settled into place
each morning.

> *Cannot see the mountains out the front door*
> *or the canyon which means that we are sitting*

> *in the middle of this big marshmallow and*
> *breathing the smoke.*

The highest peaks were moving
on the white edges
of gray clouds.

> *The evacuation is being issued as a safety*
> *precaution due to burnout operations*
> *taking place in the area south of Forest Road 42.*

Fire flowed upslope
eating the pines as it went.

> *Check lines have been put in and burnouts*
> *conducted to support the protection of populated*
> *areas just outside the wilderness.*

The afternoon winds calmed
from anger to unease
by nightfall
when the back-burn began.
The night sky melted
into valleys not even
the deer could reach.

> *Saturday has dawned and we can see the blue sky*
> *but everything else is socked in*

There was waiting for the clocks
to tick again
amid fire lines and fear,
and finally the notice
to return

Aspen Fire
Incident Type: Wildfire
Cause: Human
Date: 2003
Location: Mount Lemmon, Santa Catalina Mountains near Tucson, AZ
Size: 84,750 Acres
Vegetation: Aspen / Pine-Oak / Conifer
Management: Suppressed
Structures Lost: 325

> *Even from inside the car we heard a lot of birds*
> *in the burned areas including SULFUR-BELLIED*
> *FLYCATCHER, ACORN WOODPECKER,*
> *FLICKERS, BLACK PHOEBE...*

to what had been left behind
and to return the birds
to the trees that survived

> *PAINTED REDSTART, BLACK-THROATED GRAY*
> *WARBLER, GRACE'S WARBLER, HUTTON'S &*
> *PLUMBEOUS VIREOS, WHITE-BREASTED NUTHATCH,*
> *WESTERN WOOD PEEWEE, MEXICAN JAYS,*
> *SPOTTED TOWHEE & WESTERN and HEPATIC*
> *TANAGER. A hen turkey in stealth mode*

and see them all as if

> *was slinking along the creek probably taking a break*
> *from sitting on eggs, and chipmunks, rock squirrels and*
> *tree squirrels were around. The goshawks have hatched.*

for the first time, when

> *It was reassuring to see and hear so much life,*
> *the life that is so important to many of us personally*

it had been so close to being
the last.

(Indented sections are excerpts taken from Winston Lewis' Facebook page from the time of the Horseshoe 2 fire in the Chiricahua Mountains in 2011. The final observations, on birds returning, are messages from Helen Snyder.)

Slide Fire
Incident Type: Wildfire
Cause: Human
Date: 2014
Location: Oak Creek Canyon, North of Sedona, AZ
Size: 21,227 Acres
Vegetation: Juniper-Pinyon / Ponderosa Pine / Douglas Fir
Management: Suppressed

Fire Run

Even while flames are close
   an elk will graze,

chewing down the time
   he has to reach water

while deer leave only
   their tracks to burn

when the heat drives a snake
   into the earth

where it waits
   before sliding back to light

ahead of the coyote
   who turns into smoke

to escape before
   he re-enters his body

      always a step

         faster than fire.

Schultz Fire
Incident Type: Wildfire
Cause: Human
Date: 2010
Location: Schultz Peak, San Francisco Mountain near Flagstaff, AZ
Size: 15,075 Acres
Vegetation: Ponderosa Pine / Mixed Conifer
Management: Suppressed

Sunlight and Ashes: Forest after Fire

I

Stripped to their essentials
              where space
        opened up around them

these wounded trunks
            still occupy
the ground with their roots
growing thirty feet into
            darkness
       and sharing
              what earth feels
              when fire

has passed over it

      and the unobstructed view at night

is of the stars as they flow

between the broken

crowns.

II

After the smoke had cleared
the sky broke through
between blackened trunks,
blue shading to a pale
light above the ridge the forest
used to hide when
the trees gave cover
to the Cooper's hawk

and marked the way
deer followed to water.
Long shadows came to rest
softly on the ash
with pine needles

sprinkled across them
like pen strokes
struggling to become
a language describing

the appetite of a fire

that reached for the highest

branches, and ran

      to the edge

           of every one.

III

On a quiet day, the red formations

are solidly positioned

where they stood while flames

climbed their heights and raced into

their shady canyons.
                         The story is
that someone tossed a cigarette aside
not far from the road
where it follows yet another curve
between the forested slopes
and the fire climbed
faster than anyone could follow it.
It had no weight to slow it
as it ran,
        while the rocks
watched it pick out which trees
to burn and which to pass.
Fire is so impatient; rocks
have time to wait

for trees to grow back.

Yarnell Hill Fire
Incident Type: Wildfire
Cause: Lightning
Date: 2013
Location: Yarnell, AZ
Size: 8,500 Acres
Vegetation: Chaparral / Pinyon-Juniper Woodlands
Management: Suppressed
Structures Lost: 129
Deaths: 19

IV

On a meadow bright with Goldeneye

a black stump sticks
up among the fine green Yarrow
and Broad-leaved Mullein

that have grown two months
back through the layers
of splintered bark
and residue from a fire
that split stones open

when it had no more forest
to burn, and rippled along
the ground to lay down
beside a Wheeler's Thistle

that swayed just a little
as the last spark glowed

a second before

going dark.

V

It hasn't been long since
the pines were here,
dark green
and home to Goshawks; it hasn't taken
as long for the land to change

as it takes a child to grow
to the age of curiosity, when
he asks what kind of tree that is,
and the parent
says

    It's aspen; it grows
from a fire.

VI

Each footstep leaves
a loose print in the ashes
now cooled from
a slowly paced fire
that glowed
close to the ground
as it warmed the low bark
while smoke caressed
the branches
from which the juncos
scattered, and to which
their calls return
in gray light.

Warm Fire
Incident Type: Wildfire
Cause: Lightning
Date: 2006
Location: Kaibab Plateau, AZ
Size: 59,000 Acres
Vegetation: Mixed Conifer / Ponderosa Pine / Pinyon-Juniper Woodlands
Management: Managed; Suppressed

Forest Oracle

Seventeenth century trees
glistened in the rain
that fell frequently upon them

while saplings grew so tall
they survived the fires
that followed, and the cycle

made the forests strong
until men arrived who wanted
so much they killed every fire

it was possible to kill, but
they angered the fires
that returned in a new millennium.

Now a beetle smaller than a raindrop
can bring down a tall pine.
The forests cannot walk

to where water is
and fires move swiftly
through them. When they burn

they burn far and burn fast.
They rise and take hold
of the sky coming down

to be part of the world
they destroy. They destroy
for the thrill of destroying.

Ponderosas die without telling us why.
The land will diminish
upon which they can grow

and the seasons will be named
winter, spring, fire, and fall.
But people who have lived

many lives where the winds
come unexpectedly and speak
in consonants to the stars

are not afraid, having once heard
the sound fire makes
and joined with it in chorus.

Illustrations by Julie Comnick

Cover art, "Fire 1," by Serpentino (Hans Thoursie)

Cover and interior book design by Diane Kistner

Author photos by Jennifer Gunlock

Libre Baskerville text and titling, Arial illustrative detail

About FutureCycle Press

FutureCycle Press is dedicated to publishing lasting English-language poetry books, chapbooks, and anthologies in both print-on-demand and ebook formats. Founded in 2007 by long-time independent editor/publishers and partners Diane Kistner and Robert S. King, the press incorporated as a nonprofit in 2012. A number of our editors are distinguished poets and writers in their own right, and we have been actively involved in the small press movement going back to the early seventies.

The FutureCycle Poetry Book Prize and honorarium is awarded annually for the best full-length volume of poetry we publish in a calendar year. Introduced in 2013, our Good Works projects are anthologies devoted to issues of universal significance, with all proceeds donated to a related worthy cause. Our Selected Poems series highlights contemporary poets with a substantial body of work to their credit; with this series we strive to resurrect work that has had limited distribution and is now out of print.

We are dedicated to giving all of the authors we publish the care their work deserves, making our catalog of titles the most diverse and distinguished it can be, and paying forward any earnings to fund more great books.

We've learned a few things about independent publishing over the years. We've also evolved a unique, resilient publishing model that allows us to focus mainly on vetting and preserving for posterity the most books of exceptional quality without becoming overwhelmed with bookkeeping and mailing, fundraising activities, or taxing editorial and production "bubbles." To find out more about what we are doing, come see us at www.futurecycle.org.

www.ingramcontent.com/pod-product-compliance
Lightning Source LLC
LaVergne TN
LVHW020939090426
835512LV00020B/3432